This Book Belongs To

....

....

....

Made in the USA
Las Vegas, NV
04 December 2021